CITIZENSHIP

BY LUCIA RAATMA

CHILDREN'S PRESS®
An Imprint of Scholastic Inc.
New York Toronto London Auckland Sydney
Mexico City New Delhi Hong Kong
Danbury, Connecticut

BRINGING HISTORY to LIFE

Content Consultant
James Marten, PhD
Professor and Chair, History Department
Marquette University
Milwaukee, Wisconsin

Library of Congress Cataloging-in-Publication Data

Raatma, Lucia.
  Citizenship/by Lucia Raatma.
    p. cm.—(Cornerstones of freedom)
  Includes bibliographical references and index.
  ISBN-13: 978-0-531-23064-0 (lib. bdg.)   ISBN-10: 0-531-23064-3 (lib. bdg.)
  ISBN-13: 978-0-531-28164-2 (pbk.)   ISBN-10: 0-531-28164-7 (pbk.)
1. Citizenship—United States—Juvenile literature. I. Title. II. Series.
  JK1759.R32 2012
  323.60973—dc23   2011031340

Printed in the United States of America 113
SCHOLASTIC, CHILDREN'S PRESS, CORNERSTONES OF FREEDOM™,
and associated logos are trademarks and/or registered trademarks of
Scholastic Inc.

1 2 3 4 5 6 7 8 9 10 R 21 20 19 18 17 16 15 14 13 12

Photographs © 2012: age fotostock/Everett Collection: 38; Amos Schueller:
15; AP Images: 25 (Alan Diaz), 54, 59 (Bob Child), 8 (Damian Dovarganes),
20 (Elise Amendola), 34 (Jerry Willis/Muskogee Daily Phoenix), 42 (John
Gaps III), 14 (Kathy Willens), 50 (Ron Edmonds), 5 top, 16; Getty Images/
AFP: 17; Landov/Jason Reed/Reuters: 18; Media Bakery: 11 (Ariel
Skelley), 4 top, 12 (Roberto Westbrook), cover, 22, 35; PhotoEdit/Bonnie
Kamin: 26; Shutterstock, Inc.: 23 (Rob Marmion), back cover (Sylvana
Rega); Superstock, Inc.: 49 (imagebroker.net), 29 (Stock Connection), 40
(Underwood Photo Archives), 4 bottom, 7, 47, 57 top; The Image Works:
45 (akg-images), 28 (Allen Tannenbaum), 24 (Ann Hermes/Christian
Science Monitor), 36 (Bob Daemmrich), 48 (Charles Gatewood), 10 (Ellen
B. Senisi), 2, 3, 6, 56, 58 (Iberfoto), 55 (Jim West), 39 (Kathy McLaughlin),
41 (Kendra Helmer/Journal-Courier), 5 bottom, 30, 51 (Marjorie Kamys
Cotera/Daemmrich Photography), 13 (Mary Evans/Pharcide), 32 (Michael
Geissinger), 27 (Robert Sciarrino/The Star-Ledger), 37 (Roger-Viollet), 44
(Sipley/ClassicStock), 46 (ullstein bild); U.S. State Department: 21, 57 bottom.

Maps by XNR Productions, Inc.

Did you know that studying history can be fun?

BRING HISTORY TO LIFE by becoming a history investigator. Examine the evidence (primary and secondary source materials); cross-examine the people and witnesses. Take a look at what was happening at the time—but be careful! What happened years ago might suddenly become incredibly interesting and change the way you think!

Contents

Congress of the United States
begun and held at the City of New-York, on
Wednesday the fourth of March, one thousand seven hundred and eighty nine

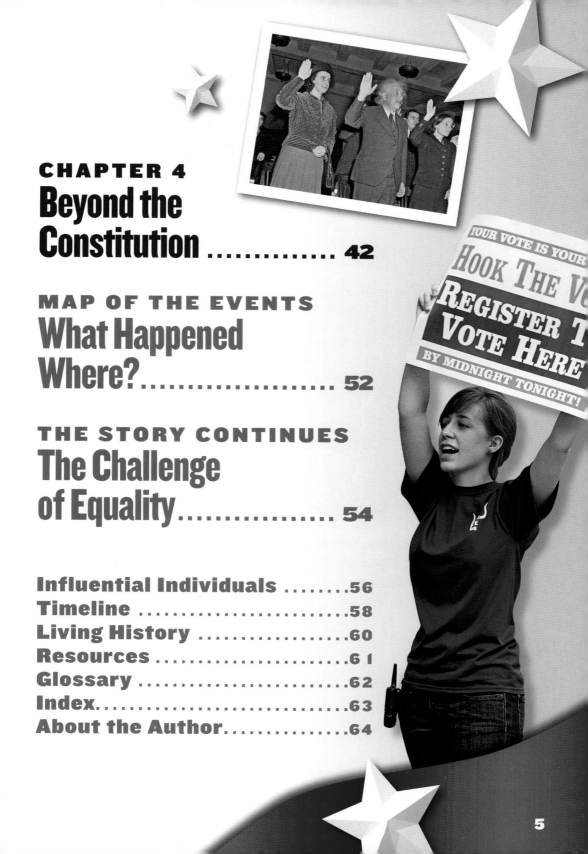

A Nation Begins

The Declaration of Independence was written by Thomas Jefferson, Benjamin Franklin, Roger Sherman, Philip Livingston, and John Adams.

"Life, liberty and the pursuit of happiness" are three rights that were written into the **Declaration of Independence**. The **Founding Fathers** of the United States believed that the colonists in North America were being denied these rights by the British government. Thomas Jefferson and other

THERE HAVE BEEN 27 AMENDMENTS

leaders wrote the Declaration of Independence in 1776, during the American Revolutionary War (1775–1783). This document stated the colonies' intention of freeing themselves from British rule.

When American forces won the revolution, a new nation was born. The newly free American people now had to create a government of their own. In 1787, leaders met and wrote the U.S. Constitution, a document that outlined the basic framework of the government.

Then in 1789, the Bill of Rights was created under the leadership of James Madison. These first 10 **amendments** to the Constitution addressed the basic rights of the U.S. people and covered important issues that the Constitution had not made clear. The Bill of Rights dealt with issues such as free speech and religion. It also included ideas about fair trials and owning property. Protecting the rights of Americans was a key factor for the new country, and it continues to be an issue today. Along with these rights, every U.S. citizen also has important responsibilities and privileges.

The Bill of Rights guarantees a set of basic rights to all U.S. citizens.

Congress of the United States

begun and held at the City of New-York, on Wednesday the fourth of March, one thousand seven hundred and eighty nine

THE Convention of a number of the states, having at the time of their adopting the Constitution, expressed a desire, in order to prevent misconstruction or abuse of its powers, that further declaratory and restrictive clauses should be added: And as extending the ground of public confidence in the Government, will best ensure the beneficent ends of its institution.

RESOLVED by the Senate and House of Representatives of the United States of America, in Congress assembled, two thirds of both Houses concurring, that the following Articles be proposed to the Legislatures of the several States, as amendments to the Constitution of the United States, all, or any of which Articles, when ratified by three fourths of the

TO THE U.S. CONSTITUTION.

which, the proportion shall be so regulated by Congress, that there shall be not less than one hundred Representatives, nor less than one Representative for every forty thousand persons, until the number of Representatives shall amount to two hundred, after which the proportion shall be so regulated by Congress, that there shall not be less than two hundred Representatives, nor more than one Representative for every fifty thousand persons.

CHAPTER 1

BEING A U.S. CITIZEN

Special ceremonies are held to welcome new U.S. citizens to the country.

HOW DOES A PERSON BECOME a U.S. citizen? Today, there are a number of ways. A person can be born in the United States. A person can also be born to U.S. citizens in another country. A third way is to move to the United States and choose to become a citizen. However, this last option is a long and serious process. It is an important decision for anyone, so there are many steps required.

Born in the USA

When a baby is born in the United States, that child is automatically a U.S. citizen. The 14th Amendment guarantees that citizenship. The child can then go to U.S. schools and do all the things that other American children do.

A baby is also considered a U.S. citizen if he or she is born in a U.S. **territory**. At least one parent must be a U.S. citizen who has lived in the United States for at least one year. Territories include Guam, the U.S. Virgin Islands, and others. People born in Puerto Rico are also considered U.S. citizens, though they cannot vote for the U.S. president.

All children born in the United States are automatically U.S. citizens.

Even though people in the military often live overseas, their children are still U.S. citizens.

Citizens in Other Countries

Sometimes U.S. citizens are in other countries when they have a baby. Maybe they are in the military and are stationed in another nation. They might work for companies that have sent them to offices in other countries. When both parents are U.S. citizens and have a baby in another country, that baby is still a U.S. citizen.

It gets more complicated if only one parent is a U.S. citizen. In that case, if that citizen has lived in the United States for at least a year, and if the other parent is a **U.S. national**, the child is a U.S. citizen. If the other parent is not a national, the child might still be a U.S. citizen. The parent who is a U.S. citizen must have lived in the United States for at least five years, two of them after age 14.

If only one parent is a U.S. citizen, the child might not be a U.S. citizen.

Coming to the United States

Throughout the history of the United States, people from other countries have wanted to **immigrate** to the nation and become citizens. Many people from all over the world came to the American colonies before the United States was created. In the 1800s and early 1900s, more people from European countries such as Italy, Ireland, and France decided to make their new homes in the United States. They often traveled by ship, arriving at harbors in such cities as Boston, Massachusetts; New York City, New York; Baltimore, Maryland; San Francisco, California; Miami, Florida; New Orleans, Louisiana; and Savannah, Georgia.

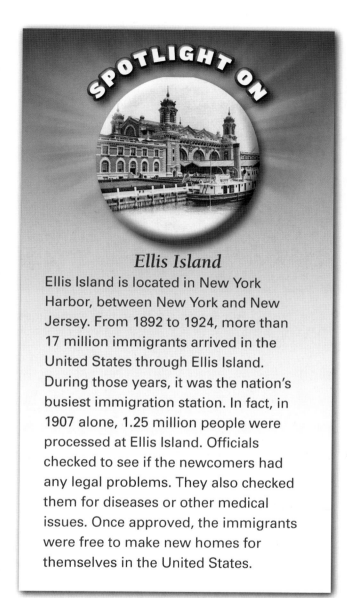

SPOTLIGHT ON

Ellis Island

Ellis Island is located in New York Harbor, between New York and New Jersey. From 1892 to 1924, more than 17 million immigrants arrived in the United States through Ellis Island. During those years, it was the nation's busiest immigration station. In fact, in 1907 alone, 1.25 million people were processed at Ellis Island. Officials checked to see if the newcomers had any legal problems. They also checked them for diseases or other medical issues. Once approved, the immigrants were free to make new homes for themselves in the United States.

Becoming a citizen can sometimes be a difficult process.

In the years since then, people from Asia, the Middle East, and other regions have come to live in the United States. Many people from bordering Canada and Mexico have also chosen the United States as their new home. However, they are not allowed to just arrive and say they are citizens. They have to go through a long process to officially receive citizenship status.

A FIRSTHAND LOOK AT
THE STATUE OF LIBERTY

In New York Harbor, near Ellis Island, stands the Statue of Liberty. A gift from the people of France in 1886, the statue honors the U.S. tradition of welcoming immigrants. Its inscription, "The New Colossus," is a message of hope for immigrants coming to America. See page 60 for a link to read the original poem online.

Becoming a U.S. Citizen

There are several steps people have to take once they decide to become U.S. citizens. They have to file an application and have their fingerprints taken. They have to take and pass a test about U.S. history and government. They must also take an English language test to prove that they can speak and read English. After that, they appear in court to tell a judge why they want to be U.S. citizens. The people who complete this process are called **naturalized** citizens.

There are certain requirements that naturalized citizens have to meet. They must be at least 18 years old, and they must have been living in the United States for at

YESTERDAY'S HEADLINES

In 1912, a Polish man named Beys Afroyim (above left) moved to the United States. He became a naturalized citizen in 1926. He later moved to Israel, became a citizen there, and voted in an Israeli election. In 1960, Afroyim decided to move back to the United States. However, he was informed that since he had voted in Israel, he could no longer be a U.S. national. He took his case to court, against U.S. Secretary of State Dean Rusk. In 1967, the Supreme Court heard the case *Afroyim v. Rusk*, and the justices ruled in favor of Afroyim. They decided that the 14th Amendment guaranteed him dual citizenship.

Albert Einstein was one of many well-known people who chose to become U.S. citizens.

least five years. They have to pass the necessary tests and pledge their loyalty to the United States.

Not every person who becomes a naturalized citizen loses citizenship in his or her original country. People who are citizens in two nations are said to have dual citizenship. The famous scientist Albert Einstein is a good example of this. He became a U.S. citizen in 1940, but he remained a citizen of Switzerland, too.

Many years ago, a person could lose U.S. citizenship if he or she became a citizen of another country or served in another country's military. Today, dual citizenship is much more accepted. However, a naturalized citizen who commits a serious crime against the United States can lose U.S. citizenship.

Former U.S. citizen Adam Gadahn lost his citizenship for helping a terrorist group attack the United States.

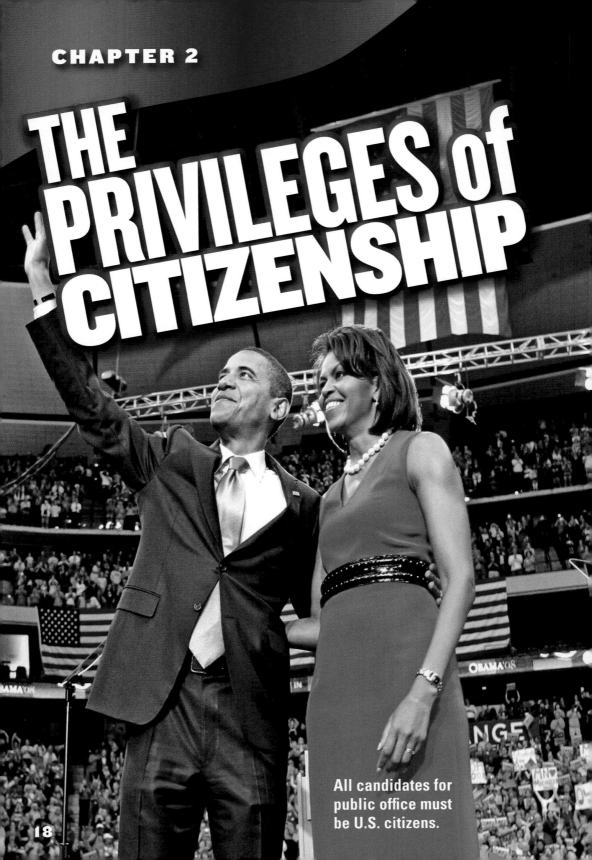

CHAPTER 2

THE PRIVILEGES of CITIZENSHIP

All candidates for public office must be U.S. citizens.

BEING A U.S. CITIZEN INVOLVES more than just living in the United States. Many people visit the United States each year, and some choose to stay for a set period of time. However, people who are citizens have certain rights and privileges that visitors or temporary residents do not have. Holding public office, having government jobs, and voting in government elections are among these rights. Other rights include being treated fairly by the courts and being treated the same as other citizens.

The winning presidential candidate must take an oath of office to become president.

Running for Office

Every year, thousands of people decide to run for public office in the United States. They may want to be mayors of their towns, members of Congress, or governors of their states. To be eligible, all these people must be U.S. citizens. They can either have been born in the United States or have become naturalized citizens.

To be president of the United States, however, a person must have been born in the United States. The U.S. Constitution states that requirement, but many lawmakers have suggested that the law should be changed. So far, all of their arguments have failed.

U.S. Citizens on Vacation

When people travel from country to country, they have to show their passports. These documents are forms of identification. They are also symbols of citizenship. U.S. citizens and nationals travel with U.S. passports, which guarantee the right to return to the United States. Passports are also used if U.S. citizens need help in foreign countries, such as if they are charged with crimes. They can go to U.S. embassies located in those countries and show their passports. Then workers at the embassy can help with whatever problem the travelers are having. People with dual citizenship are required to use their U.S. passports when they leave or enter the United States.

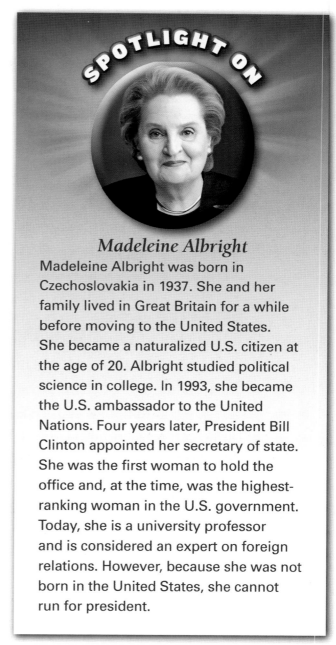

SPOTLIGHT ON

Madeleine Albright

Madeleine Albright was born in Czechoslovakia in 1937. She and her family lived in Great Britain for a while before moving to the United States. She became a naturalized U.S. citizen at the age of 20. Albright studied political science in college. In 1993, she became the U.S. ambassador to the United Nations. Four years later, President Bill Clinton appointed her secretary of state. She was the first woman to hold the office and, at the time, was the highest-ranking woman in the U.S. government. Today, she is a university professor and is considered an expert on foreign relations. However, because she was not born in the United States, she cannot run for president.

A FIRSTHAND LOOK AT
PRESIDENT OBAMA'S BIRTH CERTIFICATE

President Barack Obama was elected to office in 2008. He was born in Hawaii to a mother who was a U.S. citizen and a father from Kenya. Some people questioned whether Hawaii was really his place of birth, so in 2011 he released his official birth certificate to the public. This proved that he was born in one of the 50 states and was eligible to be president. See page 60 for a link to view the birth certificate online.

On the Job

In the United States, people hold all kinds of jobs. Some people work for big companies, while others start businesses of their own. Some people work for the government. Government employees work at post offices, in government offices, and on military bases. People who are U.S. citizens have the right to apply for

U.S. citizens can own businesses and work a wide variety of jobs.

U.S. citizens are protected against discrimination when applying for jobs.

and hold these jobs. People who are not citizens are not allowed to work many jobs in the United States unless they get special permission from the government.

U.S. citizens and authorized foreign workers are protected by the U.S. government, no matter what kind of business they work for. For instance, companies have to follow laws about fair hiring. They have to follow rules about offering health insurance and family leave. Companies are not allowed to fire employees based on gender, race, or other personal factors.

Rights of Speech and Property

The U.S. Bill of Rights focuses on some key privileges for U.S. citizens. One of the most important is the right to free speech. This means that citizens can always voice their opinions, even if they are criticizing the government or its leaders. Part of free speech is the right to protest peacefully. Citizens are allowed to gather and march for issues that are important to them. They cannot be arrested for what they think or say. This is not true around the world. In some countries, a person can be put in jail for saying the wrong thing about the government or a leader.

The Bill of Rights guarantees that all U.S. citizens can hold protests as long as the protests do not become violent.

U.S. citizens participate in a wide variety of religions.

Freedom of religion is another key privilege. Before American independence, many people had come to the colonies to avoid limitations and bans on their religions in Europe. The Founding Fathers believed that no religion should be officially supported by the government. In the United States today, there are people of many faiths, including Christianity, Judaism, Buddhism, Islam, and Hinduism. There are also people who choose not to practice any religion at all.

Another important right involves property. The Bill of Rights ensures that the military or the government cannot take property owned by U.S. citizens without first taking the proper legal action to make sure the citizens' rights are not violated. There are also laws that prevent the government from searching citizens' property without good reason.

Police officers are not allowed to search a citizen's home without permission from a judge.

In the Courts

Everywhere in the world there are people who break the law. Some people have to go to jail or pay a fine for the crimes they have committed. However, in the United

States, the courts consider all people to be innocent until they are proven guilty. This ensures that U.S. citizens receive a fair trial in the court system, no matter what they have been accused of.

In some countries, people who are accused of crimes might appear before only a judge or a government leader. They could be sent to jail or even punished with death, without any sort of trial. In the United States, people are guaranteed the right to tell their side of the story and to be represented by a lawyer in court. Often, a jury listens to both sides of a court case. This group of citizens then decides if the accused person is guilty or not. This way, one person alone does not decide the fate of another.

All U.S. citizens accused of crimes have the right to a fair trial and the help of a lawyer.

YESTERDAY'S HEADLINES

In 1995, Timothy McVeigh (above) committed a terrible crime. He set off a bomb just outside a federal building in Oklahoma City, Oklahoma. His actions killed 168 people and hurt more than 500 others. Some of the victims were children in a day care center. After McVeigh was arrested, he was accused of many crimes including murder. Before his trial began, officials realized he could not get a fair trial in Oklahoma, where many of the victims had lived. So his trial was moved to Denver, Colorado. Eventually, McVeigh was found guilty and sentenced to death. However, as a U.S. citizen he received a fair trial.

In the Voting Booth

Another important privilege of U.S. citizenship is the right to vote. Every U.S. citizen age 18 or older is eligible to vote in local, state, and national elections. Registering to vote is easy. The main requirements for people who register to vote are proving their citizenship and showing where they live. When they move from neighborhood to neighborhood or state to state, voters are required to register under their new addresses. This ensures that they don't vote in the wrong places. Local governments are in charge of making sure citizens are properly registered.

By having the right to vote, U.S. citizens have a voice in the U.S. government. They can vote for the mayor of their town and for other people to hold local offices. They can also vote for members of Congress, the governors of their states, and the president of the United States.

Voting is both a right and a responsibility.

CHAPTER 3

THE RESPONSIBILITIES OF CITIZENSHIP

Some citizens help the country by encouraging others to vote.

HOOK THE VOTE

YOUR VOICE

REGISTER TO VOTE HERE

BY MIDNIGHT TONIGHT!

IN ADDITION TO HAVING rights and privileges, U.S. citizens also have many responsibilities. These responsibilities are necessary to keep a democratic government running smoothly. To be good citizens, people should have the best interests of their nation in mind. They should want to keep their country strong, and they should ensure that all people are treated fairly. They can work toward this goal in a number of ways. They can vote in elections, serve on juries, obey laws, and serve in the military. They can be responsible citizens by becoming involved in their community and trying to make it a better place.

Large numbers of people turn out to vote on election days.

The Duty of Voting

Voting is certainly a right of U.S. citizenship, but it is also more than that. In many people's minds, voting is a duty. Citizens may not agree with everything that the U.S. government does, and they may not like every elected official. However, if they do not vote, they are missing out on their opportunity to play a role in the government. Voting is a critical way for citizens to make their opinions known.

Voters are also responsible for learning all they can about candidates and understanding important political issues. That way, they are informed when they cast their votes.

In some countries, there are no public elections. Instead, the leaders make all the decisions and give their people no voice. Voting helps citizens become part of the government process.

Jury Duty

All U.S. citizens accused of crimes are guaranteed the right to a trial by jury. These juries are made up of other U.S. citizens. Throughout the United States, thousands of people are called to jury duty each week. That means they are told to appear at a courthouse to be evaluated to serve on a jury. During the evaluation process, lawyers and judges ask the people questions about their

A VIEW FROM ABROAD

Many people in Afghanistan have risked their lives to vote in recent elections. In 2004, Afghanistan held its first free election. Between five million and seven million people stood in long lines and voted. Since then, the voting numbers have been lower. Members of the Taliban, a **terrorist** group, threatened to hurt or kill people who voted in the 2010 election. "There's nothing to be afraid of," Governor Tooryalai Wesa said to the Afghan people. "The enemy wants the election to fail, so if you want the [terrorists] out of your land, you'll have to come out and vote."

personal lives and the work they do. These questions help determine if the citizens could listen to a court case and fairly decide if a person is guilty of a crime or not.

A jury usually has 12 people, and it should represent people of many backgrounds. The group chooses a leader, called a foreman or forewoman. This leader helps the jury stay focused and may also send questions to the judge. Jury members listen to both sides in a trial. They hear about the crime that occurred and how the victims were affected. They also learn about the person accused of the crime. Some trials take just a few days. Others can take weeks, months, or even years.

Potential jurors must register once they arrive at the courthouse.

Jurors must pay careful attention to everything that happens in a trial.

Some people try to avoid jury duty. They do not want to lose time from their work or their family. However, serving on a jury is an important part of being a good citizen. Juries play important roles in keeping innocent people out of jail, punishing people who commit crimes, and protecting the rights of victims.

In the Military

U.S. citizens are eligible to serve in the U.S. military. The military is made up of the U.S. Army, Air Force, Navy, Marines, and Coast Guard. Each branch of the military has different responsibilities in defending the United States and protecting its citizens. Most members of the military join because they want to. They may want to serve their country for a few years, or they may see the military as an important career.

The military helps protect the country from threats.

Many U.S. citizens were drafted and sent to fight in Korea during the Korean War.

There are times, however, when military service is not a choice. During wartimes, a draft may be required. This means that male citizens age 18 and older can be called upon to serve in the military. The draft has been used a number of times throughout U.S. history, including during the Civil War (1861–1865), World War I (1914–1918), World War II (1939–1945), the Korean War (1950–1953), and the Vietnam War (1955–1975).

A FIRSTHAND LOOK AT
ANTIWAR PROTESTS

During the Vietnam War, many U.S. citizens disagreed with the draft. Some men left the United States and went to other countries. Others burned their draft cards in protest. Citizens across the country participated in protests against the war and the draft. See page 60 for a link to view newspapers, photos, and other antiwar materials online.

The Vietnam War inspired massive protests throughout the United States.

During many of these wars, some citizens did not think the United States should be involved in the conflict. Some of them protested the draft. Many college students held marches against the Vietnam War. The Bill of Rights guaranteed their rights to free speech and peaceful protest. Some young men refused to join the military, even when they were drafted. They left the United States and moved to other countries. In this case, these men were denying their responsibilities as U.S. citizens and breaking the law.

Today, there is not a draft in place. However, men who are ages 18 to 25 are required to register with the Selective Service. This system gives the government the names of eligible men to call upon if military service is suddenly needed.

Many high school students choose to join the military after graduating.

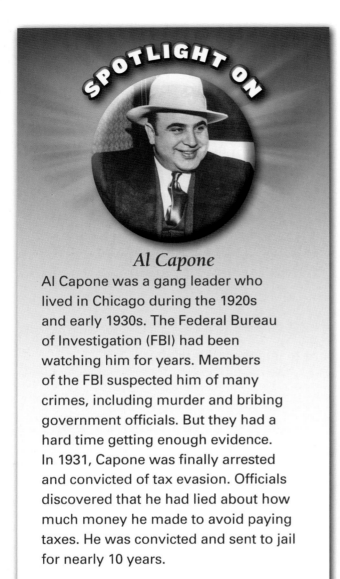

SPOTLIGHT ON

Al Capone

Al Capone was a gang leader who lived in Chicago during the 1920s and early 1930s. The Federal Bureau of Investigation (FBI) had been watching him for years. Members of the FBI suspected him of many crimes, including murder and bribing government officials. But they had a hard time getting enough evidence. In 1931, Capone was finally arrested and convicted of tax evasion. Officials discovered that he had lied about how much money he made to avoid paying taxes. He was convicted and sent to jail for nearly 10 years.

Obeying the Law

U.S. citizens are expected to obey the laws of their towns, states, and the nation. If they break laws, they may have to pay fines or go to jail. For instance, a person who drives too fast might have to appear in court and pay money to the community. But a person who robs a store might be sentenced to prison. Some people who commit serious crimes can go to jail and lose the right to vote.

An important law for all citizens is the requirement to pay **taxes**. Some people do not like the idea that the government takes part of their income. However, many government programs rely on taxes. Money from taxes is used to pay for schools and teachers. It is also used to build roads and bridges, and it helps pay for the military. People who do not pay the required taxes can face fines or even time in jail.

Volunteers help make sure that dogs at animal shelters get their daily exercise.

Community Involvement

Being a good citizen is about obeying the law and voting, but it's also about being involved in the community. Responsible citizens report crimes that they witness. They watch out for problems in their neighborhoods. They attend school board meetings and help with local fund-raisers. They may volunteer their time at hospitals and animal shelters. U.S. citizens show their involvement by cleaning up local parks, recycling bottles and cans, and picking up roadside litter. The most important thing a U.S. citizen can do is help make the nation the best place it can be.

CHAPTER 4

BEYOND the CONSTITUTION

Riots broke out in Los Angeles, California, in 1992 after an all-white jury returned a verdict of not guilty for four white police officers accused of brutality against a black man.

IN THE DECLARATION OF Independence, Thomas Jefferson and the other Founding Fathers stated that "all men are created equal." They meant that all citizens are equal in importance to government leaders and that all people should have a voice in the government. Equality was an important foundation for this nation. The 14th and 15th Amendments guaranteed equal rights for people of all races. Over the years, some U.S. citizens have not been treated equally, however. State and local governments have denied fair trials, voting rights, and freedom of speech. Many people have lost their lives fighting for the rights they are entitled to.

Slavery was a common practice in the early history of the United States.

Equal Rights?

Throughout U.S. history, there are instances of rights being denied. For example, for nearly 200 years, people of African background were enslaved. They were bought and sold as property. Some of the Founding Fathers even owned slaves. It took decades for slavery to be legally declared inhumane and unacceptable. Slavery finally ended with the 13th Amendment to the Constitution in 1865.

Even after being freed from slavery, many African Americans were denied equal rights throughout the United States. In some states, they were not given equal voting rights. In some of these same states, Jim Crow laws were enforced. These laws were forms of **segregation**, meant to keep black Americans separate from white Americans. There were white and black sections in movie theaters and restaurants. There were separate waiting rooms at train stations. There were even separate drinking fountains.

African Americans were also denied equal education through segregated schools. This practice remained in place until 1954. That year, the Supreme Court ruled in *Brown v. Board of Education of Topeka, Kansas*

Businesses such as movie theaters were often separated by race.

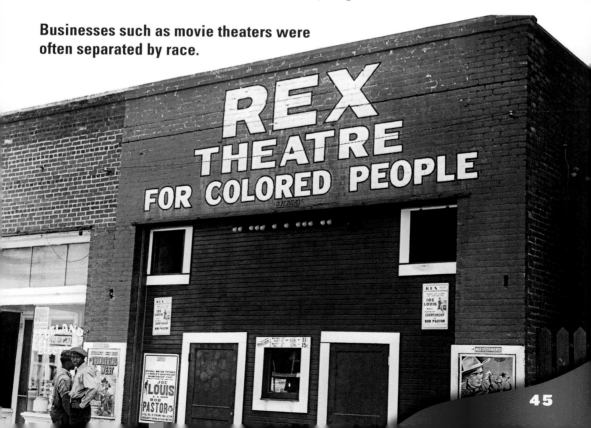

that separate schools were unconstitutional. But the process to end segregation was slow and marked by violence. Many people objected to white and black Americans attending the same schools. In Arkansas in 1957, Governor Orval Faubus used the state's National Guard to block African American students from entering Little Rock High School. President Dwight Eisenhower responded by sending in the federal military to protect the students.

In the 1950s and 1960s, the **civil rights** movement helped African Americans obtain the rights they deserved. Some people marched for voting rights. Others held sit-ins, refusing to leave restaurants that practiced segregation. In Montgomery, Alabama, African

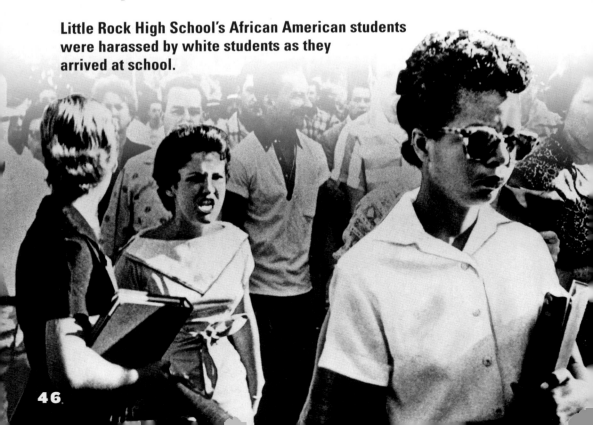

Little Rock High School's African American students were harassed by white students as they arrived at school.

Americans refused to ride on city buses. This was a reaction to the arrest of Rosa Parks, an African American woman who refused to give up her bus seat to a white man. As people around the nation and the world began to take notice, things changed for the better. Eventually, the Civil Rights Act was passed in 1964. It proved to be an important step toward real equality.

A Woman's Place

Throughout U.S. history, women have also been denied equal rights. They did not receive the right to vote until the 19th Amendment to the Constitution was passed in 1920. And over the years, they have made less money doing the same jobs that men do. In 1921, Alice Paul wrote the Equal Rights Amendment (ERA). She presented

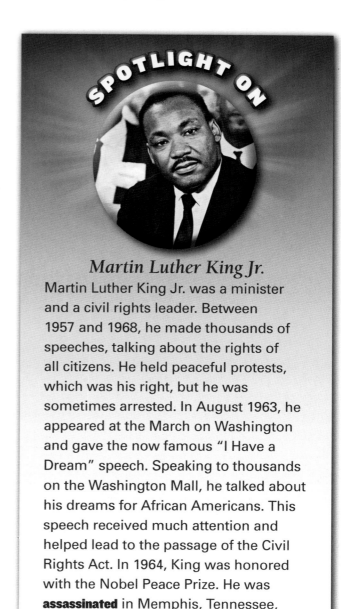

SPOTLIGHT ON

Martin Luther King Jr.

Martin Luther King Jr. was a minister and a civil rights leader. Between 1957 and 1968, he made thousands of speeches, talking about the rights of all citizens. He held peaceful protests, which was his right, but he was sometimes arrested. In August 1963, he appeared at the March on Washington and gave the now famous "I Have a Dream" speech. Speaking to thousands on the Washington Mall, he talked about his dreams for African Americans. This speech received much attention and helped lead to the passage of the Civil Rights Act. In 1964, King was honored with the Nobel Peace Prize. He was **assassinated** in Memphis, Tennessee, in 1968.

The ERA achieved a great deal of support, but was never ratified.

it to Congress two years later. This amendment would have outlawed any **discrimination** based on gender. The amendment was passed by Congress during the 1970s and 1980s, but it was never **ratified** by enough states to make it an amendment. Today, women have important jobs and have great influence in the United States, but for many it has been a difficult journey.

Debating Citizens' Rights

Some rights and privileges are hard to protect. For instance, the Bill of Rights ensures people the right of privacy. As technology changes, protecting a citizen's privacy becomes more difficult. In the age of Facebook and the Internet, people's private lives can be easily accessed.

After the terrorist attacks on September 11, 2001, national security was increased. One result was the passage of the USA PATRIOT Act. The name stands for Uniting and Strengthening America by Providing Appropriate Tools Required to Intercept and Obstruct Terrorism. It is often simply called the Patriot Act. This law allows law

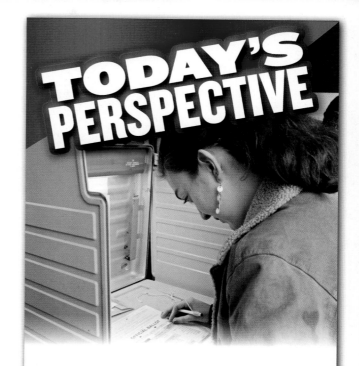

TODAY'S PERSPECTIVE

In today's world, women are mayors and governors. They serve in Congress, and they run for president. But less than 100 years ago, women were not even allowed to vote. It took leaders such as Susan B. Anthony, Elizabeth Cady Stanton, and Alice Paul to change that. They held marches and organized protests, getting the attention of the United States and the world. Their efforts finally paid off when the 19th Amendment was approved in 1920. These days, more than half of U.S. voters are women.

The USA PATRIOT Act was passed in 2001, and President George W. Bush signed a renewal on March 9, 2006.

enforcement agencies more access to personal phone calls, medical and bank records, and other private information. The idea is that this access will give officials more power to find and arrest people who want to harm the United States. Critics say that the Patriot Act violates personal privacy and is unconstitutional.

Another issue under debate involves gun rights. The Second Amendment guarantees the right to bear arms. But there is debate over what this means exactly. Many citizens feel strongly that the amendment means they

The U.S. Constitution, the Bill of Rights, and the Declaration of Independence are the three documents on which the United States was founded. They are on permanent display in the Rotunda for the Charters of Freedom at the National Archives Building in Washington, D.C. See page 60 for a link to view the documents online.

should be allowed to own guns to protect themselves. Others disagree. Some lawmakers argue that laws about gun ownership should be stronger. They believe that some people should not own guns at all and that some types of guns should not be available to private citizens. No doubt, there are some rights that will be debated for many years to come.

Some citizens believe that the Constitution guarantees the right to carry guns.

MAP OF THE EVENTS
What Happened Where?

Jersey City

Hudson River

Ellis Island In the late 19th and early 20th centuries, millions of immigrants passed through Ellis Island on their way into the United States.

Statue of Liberty The Statue of Liberty was a gift from France in 1886. It stands on Liberty Island near Ellis Island and was often the first thing immigrants saw as they entered New York Harbor.

Ellis Island

Liberty Island

Statue of Liberty

N
W   E
S

Upper New York Bay

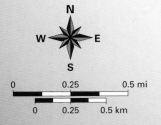

0   0.25   0.5 mi

0   0.25   0.5 km

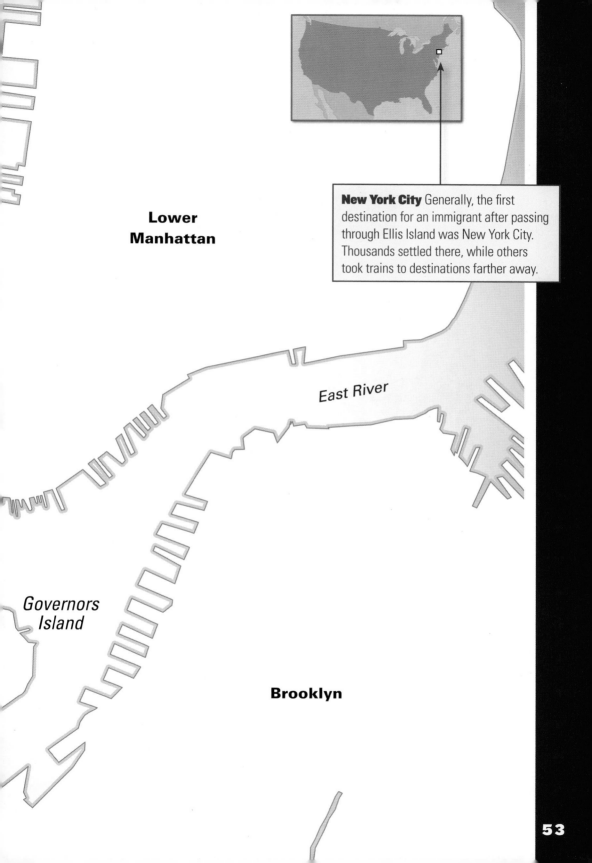

Lower Manhattan

New York City Generally, the first destination for an immigrant after passing through Ellis Island was New York City. Thousands settled there, while others took trains to destinations farther away.

East River

Governors Island

Brooklyn

The Challenge of Equality

Muslims have often been treated unfairly since the events of September 11, 2001. Here, a group marches to show their love of the United States and antiterrorism stance.

Today, for the most part, U.S. citizens can vote and speak freely. Laws protect them, and they are treated fairly in the courts. But even in the 21st century, the challenge of equality remains.

Many African Americans still experience discrimination. They may feel mistreated by employers, law enforcement, and other citizens.

After the terrorist attacks of September 11, 2001, many Americans became afraid of people from the Middle East. Since the terrorists practiced Islam, some people feared Muslim Americans. This fear has led to discrimination at schools and offices and in cities throughout the United States.

Many states continue to debate the rights of gay Americans. Many people believe that men should be allowed to marry men, and women to marry women. Other people believe that marriage should be defined as a joining of one man and one woman. As of July 2011, six states and the District of Columbia have made gay marriages legal.

The U.S. Pledge of Allegiance ends "with liberty and justice for all." This describes what the United States strives to achieve. Sometimes achieving that goal is challenging for the government and its people. As the United States continues to grow and change, so will the rights of its citizens.

Gay citizens still struggle for equal rights in most parts of the country.

WAS ORIGINALLY WRITTEN IN 1892.

INFLUENTIAL INDIVIDUALS

Thomas Jefferson

George Washington (1732–1799) was the first president of the United States and is often called the Father of His Country.

Thomas Jefferson (1743–1826) was the third president of the United States. He was the main author of the Declaration of Independence.

James Madison (1751–1836) was the fourth president of the United States and one of the Founding Fathers. He was the main author of the U.S. Constitution and led the effort to create a U.S. Bill of Rights.

Elizabeth Cady Stanton (1815–1902) was a social activist who worked to end slavery and to help women gain equal rights.

Susan B. Anthony (1820–1906) worked to help women win the right to vote in the United States. In 1872, she was arrested for voting illegally. Anthony died before the 19th Amendment was passed.

Alice Paul (1885–1977) was a leader in the women's rights movement and worked to ensure the passage of the 19th Amendment. She wrote the original Equal Rights Amendment in 1921 and proposed it to Congress in 1923.

Dwight Eisenhower (1890–1969) was the 34th president of the United States. In 1957, he sent federal troops to Arkansas to protect African American students who were entering Little Rock High School.

Beys Afroyim (1893–1984) held dual citizenship in the United States and Israel. In 1967, the Supreme Court ruled that he did not have to give up his U.S. citizenship after voting in Israel.

Al Capone (1899–1947) was a gangster who was suspected of many crimes, including murder and bribing public officials. He was finally arrested and put in jail for not paying his taxes.

Martin Luther King Jr.

Orval Faubus (1910–1994) was governor of Arkansas from 1955 to 1967. In 1957, he tried to block African American students from attending Little Rock High School.

Rosa Parks (1913–2005) was a social activist. Her arrest for not giving her bus seat to a white man helped bring attention to the civil rights movement.

Martin Luther King Jr. (1929–1968) was a minister and civil rights leader who worked to ensure that all U.S. citizens are treated equally. He received the Nobel Peace Prize and today is remembered with a federal holiday in January.

Madeleine Albright

Madeleine Albright (1937–) served as U.S. ambassador to the United Nations and was the first woman to be U.S. secretary of state. She is a naturalized citizen who was born in Czechoslovakia.

Barack Obama (1961–) is the 44th president of the United States. He proved his eligibility to be president by showing his birth certificate, which indicated that he had been born in Hawaii.

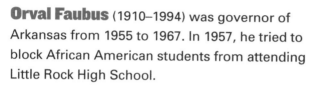

TIMELINE

1776

The Declaration of Independence is signed.

1787

The leaders at the Constitutional Convention write the U.S. Constitution.

1789

The first draft of the U.S. Bill of Rights is written.

1920

The 19th Amendment is passed, giving women the right to vote.

1954

The Supreme Court hears *Brown v. Board of Education of Topeka, Kansas* and ends segregation.

1964

The Civil Rights Act is passed.

1865

The 13th Amendment is passed, outlawing slavery in the United States.

1886

The people of France give the Statue of Liberty to the United States.

1907

In one year, 1.25 million immigrants pass through Ellis Island.

1967

The Supreme Court hears *Afroyim v. Rusk* and upholds dual citizenship.

2001

The Patriot Act is passed, allowing government agencies more access to citizens' private information.

LIVING HISTORY

Primary sources provide firsthand evidence about a topic. Witnesses to a historical event create primary sources. They include autobiographies, newspaper reports of the time, oral histories, photographs, and memoirs. A secondary source analyzes primary sources, and is one step or more removed from the event. Secondary sources include textbooks, encyclopedias, and commentaries.

Antiwar and Radical History Project—Pacific Northwest: Photos & Documents
The University of Washington at Seattle houses a large collection of anti–Vietnam War materials. Included are protest posters and buttons, photos, and newspapers. To view the collection online, visit *http://depts.washington.edu/antiwar/vietnam_intro.shtml*

The Charters of Freedom
The United States was founded on the U.S. Constitution, the Bill of Rights, and the Declaration of Independence. These three documents are on permanent display in the Rotunda for the Charters of Freedom at the National Archives Building in Washington, D.C. You can also view the documents online at *www.archives.gov/nae/visit/rotunda.html*

President Obama's Birth Certificate
In April 2011, President Barack Obama released his birth certificate to the press, showing that he had been born in Hawaii. Copies of the birth certificate are available, but the original remains at the Hawaii Department of Health. To see a copy, visit *www.whitehouse.gov/blog/2011/04/27/president-obamas-long-form-birth-certificate*

The Statue of Liberty
This monument stands in New York Harbor. "The New Colossus," a poem written by Emma Lazarus, is featured on a bronze plaque inside the Statue of Liberty's pedestal. The original handwritten poem is kept at the American Jewish Historical Society in New York City. To read the poem online, visit *www.nycinsiderguide.com/Statue-of-Liberty-Inscription.html#axzz1QOPuH72a*

RESOURCES

Books

Burgan, Michael. *The U.S. Constitution*. New York: Children's Press, 2012.

Dougherty, Terri. *Freedom of Expression and the Internet*. Detroit: Lucent Books, 2010.

Pavlovic, Zoran. *Terrorism and Security*. New York: Chelsea House, 2009.

Raatma, Lucia. *The Bill of Rights*. New York: Children's Press, 2012.

Zeiger, Jennifer. *The Civil Rights Movement*. New York: Children's Press, 2012.

Web Sites

Constitution of the United States
www.archives.gov/exhibits/charters/constitution.html
This site provides the entire text of the Constitution, along with all its amendments.

Kids.gov—Government: Citizens' Rights and Responsibilities
www.kids.gov/6_8/6_8_government_rights.shtml
This site offers links to citizenship information, including the election process, immigration, and citizens' rights.

Library of Congress: The Bill of Rights
www.loc.gov/rr/program/bib/ourdocs/billofrights.html
This site provides a background for the Bill of Rights and links to a number of related primary documents.

Visit this Scholastic Web site for more information on citizenship:
www.factsfornow.scholastic.com

GLOSSARY

amendments (uh-MEND-muhnts) changes that are made to a law or legal document

assassinated (uh-SASS-uh-nay-ted) murdered, usually someone well–known

civil rights (SIV-il RITES) the individual rights that all members of society have, including freedom and equal treatment under the law

Declaration of Independence (dek-luh-RAY-shuhn UHV in-di-PEN-duhnss) a document that declared the freedom of the 13 colonies from British rule

discrimination (diss-krim-uh-NAY-shuhn) unfair treatment of others based on age, race, gender, or other factors

Founding Fathers (FOUND-ihng FAH-thurz) the leading figures in the creation of the United States

immigrate (IM-uh-grate) to move from one country to live permanently in another

naturalized (NACH-ur-uh-lized) describing a person who was born in one country but has earned citizenship in another

ratified (RAT-uh-fyed) agreed to or approved officially

segregation (seg-ruh-GAY-shuhn) the act of separating people based on race, gender, or other factors

taxes (TAKS-uz) money that people and businesses must pay to support a government

territory (TAIR-uh-tor-ee) an area connected with or owned by a country that is outside the country's main borders

terrorist (TARE-ur-ist) a person who uses violence to frighten people, obtain power, or force a government to do something

U.S. national (YOO ESS NASH-uh-nuhl) a person who was born in another country but completes the process of earning citizenship in the United States

INDEX

Page numbers in *italics* indicate illustrations.

ABOUT THE AUTHOR

Lucia Raatma earned a bachelor's degree from the University of South Carolina and a master's degree from New York University. She has authored dozens of books for young readers and particularly enjoys writing about American history. She tries to vote in every election, and she appreciates her right of free speech. For more information, visit *www.luciaraatma.com*